SANTA'S PANTS ARE FALLING DOWN

And other SILLY SONGS of the SEASON

By Barbara Rittenhouse and
Leigh Anna Reichenbach

illustrated by Jared Lee

Scholastic Inc.

New York   Toronto   London   Auckland   Sydney
Mexico City   New Delhi   Hong Kong   Buenos Aires

For Fritz and Frank, Amanda and Alex
—B. R. and L.A.R.

To Santa Claus, who lives within us all.
—J. L.

With special thanks to Katherine Hughes, Laura Wight,
Tamar Mays, Gina Shaw, and Rachel Lisberg

ISBN 0-439-68077-8

12 11 10 9 8 7 6 5 4 3 2   4 5 6 7 8 9 /0

Printed in the U.S.A.
First printing, December 2004

CONTENTS

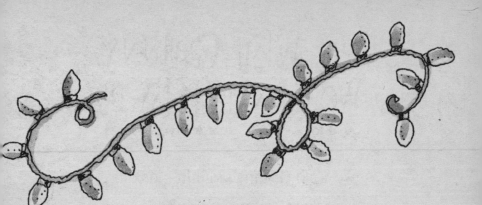

FAMILIES
Are Funny

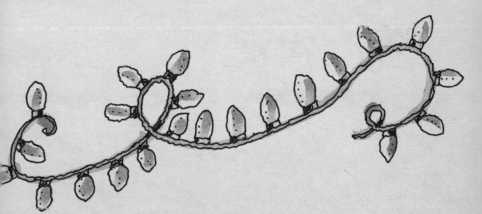

WE WISH GRANNY WOULDN'T KISS US

Sung to: We Wish You a Merry Christmas

We wish Granny wouldn't kiss us,
We wish Granny wouldn't kiss us,
We wish Granny wouldn't kiss us
Ev'ry time she comes near!

Good presents she brings,
Along with advice.
Good presents she brings us,
But they're not worth the price!

We wish Granny wouldn't hug us,
We wish Granny wouldn't hug us,
We wish Granny wouldn't hug us
'Cause her lipstick might smear.

Good gracious she's back!
Won't leave us alone.
Good gracious…good riddance!
Why won't she go home?!

OVER THE RIVER AND THROUGH THE WOODS

Sung to: Over the River and Through the Woods

Over the river and through the woods
In our SUV we go!
My dad likes to ride with me by his side
In the wind and in the snow—oh!

Up on the sidewalk and o'er the curbs
And now he's on the grass!
I'll hold on tight because tonight
He's driving way too fast!

We just missed a pothole—and swerved around
I'm feeling kinda sick.
I hope, me oh my, the next car we buy
My mother gets to pi—ick!

Thank goodness he's stopping, now I can breathe
We're finally safe at last.
Uh-oh—no way! We need a sleigh!
We just ran out of gas!

CAR TRIP

Sung to: We Three Kings

Hate these trips—
They take much too long.
Mom and Dad
Start singing dumb songs.
Dad's off-key,
and Mom's singing har-mo-ny.
Both have the words all wrong.

Oh, oh—ev'ry year we travel far.
Dad brings out his gross cigar.
It's combusting
And disgusting
Stuck inside this stupid car!

The dog just made a terrible smell.
Made me nauseous—don't feel so well.
Was it cheese?
Ugh—OPEN the window please!!
What a sad tale to tell.

Oh, oh—now there's slush and freezing sleet.
No room here to stretch my feet.
Sister's wailing—
Now it's hailing—
And we've barely left our street!

A GIFT FOR MY SISTER

Sung to: O, Little Town of Bethlehem

Oh, little sister, Beth,
I have no present yet for you.
I'm at the store in aisle four and
wondering what to do.
The pink and purple boxes are giving me a rash.
I turn and run to aisle one—
that's where I'll spend my cash!

It's finally Christmas morning, Beth,
I hope that you like my gift —
An alien with slimy skin and legs you can move and shift.
So now I'll open my gift—the one you bought for me.
A doll in braids. . . let's make a trade. . .
I hope you will agree!

WHY SPOIL THE FUN?
An Original Poem

My little brother asked today
With big and watery eyes. . .
What would Santa bring him?
Would it be a big surprise?

I told him not to worry.
I'm sure you will agree.
Why let him know this early
That the gifts are all for ME?!

OOPS!

Sung to: Pop Goes the Weasel

Grandpa ate a little too much,

He couldn't pass up nut-tin'

Now he's fast asleep in his chair . . .

POP! Goes his button!

MERRY CHRISTMAS FROM THE JOHNSONS

Sung to: Ode to Joy

Taking Christmas pictures with my family,
I hate to do.
We wear matching outfits that look goofy—
here are just a few:
Tie-dyed shirts and footie pajamas,
leis from Hawaii, cowboy hats.
And my mother even sews some clothing
for our family cats.

With the camera resting on a surface
where it's bound to fall,
Dad puts on the auto-timer and runs back
to join us all.
Brother's crying, baby is stinky,
both of the cats are scratching me.
Next year, can't we just send cards?
Just think how easy that would be!

NO ROOM FOR ONE MORE GUEST

Sung to: God Rest Ye Merry Gentlemen

God rest you merry gentlemen,
but please not in my house.
There is a fine hotel nearby that's quiet as a mouse.
My house is bursting at the seams,
and something's gotta give—
There's no room for another relative . . . re-la-tive,
There's no roo-oom for another relative.

Aunt Bertha's sleeping in my bed,
along with Uncle John.
Aunt Trudy's in the basement 'cause she
brought her dog along.
My sister and my cousin share
the trundle bed upstairs,
And they giggle all night, and no one cares . . .

it isn't fair! (spoken)

And they gi-ig-gle all night, and no one cares.

My grandmother is stiff and sore from
sleeping on the couch.
And Grandpa's in the attic room because
he's such a grouch.
And last night was the worst-est night
that I have ever had
'Cause I'm sleeping 'tween Mom
and snoring Dad . . . snoring Dad,
'Cause I'm slee-eeping 'tween Mom and snoring Dad!

WHEN MY AUNTS COME VISITING

Sung to: When the Saints Go Marching In

Oh, when my aunts
Come vis-it-ing,
Oh, when my aunts come vis-it-ing,
They yell so loud, it bursts my eardrums. . . .
When my aunts come vis-it-ing.

They scream and laugh
Those loud guffaws,
The ones that wake up all the neighbors.
I wish that Santa had brought earplugs
For when my aunts come vis-it-ing.

UP ON THE HOUSETOP

Sung to: Up on the Housetop

Up on the housetop, what's that sound?
Sounds like reindeer prancing 'round.
Everyone else here is tucked in bed.
In their excitement, I've not been fed.

Woof woof woof!
Get off the roof!
Woof woof woof!
Get off the roof!

Hey! They left cookies
Yum yum yum!
I'm going over to get me some!

I turn around as I lick my paws—
Find that I'm staring at Santa Claus
He meets my smile with a knowin
Then puts my name in his "nau

Bow wow wow!
Who's sorry now?
Bow wow wow!
No presents now.

He's up the chimney just like that!
Guess in the morning, I'll blame the cat!

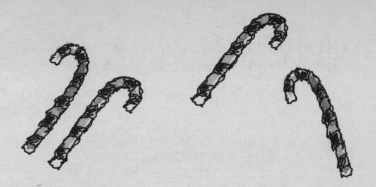

WHAT'S Cookin'?

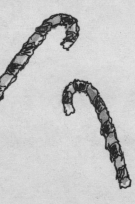

CHRISTMAS COOKIES

Sung to: Deck the Halls

Gonna bake some Christmas cookies...

Fa-la-la-la-la...Hurrah! Hooray!

Find a cookbook...take a lookie

Fa-la-la-la-la...What does it say?

Start with sugar, lots of butter...

Mix it up, mix it up...v-rum, v-rum, v-rum!

Find the flour amidst the clutter...

Toss it in the mixture...yum, yum, yum!

Roll the dough upon the table...
Roly-poly-dough...we press, press, press!
Cut the shapes out if you're able...
Sticky-sticky-gooey...what a mess!
Next the sprinkles scatter 'round us...
Shake-a-shake, shake-a-shake...
one, two, three!
Mom is surely gonna ground us...
'Cause we should have asked her first, you see!

THE GINGERBREAD MAN

Sung to: On Top of Old Smokey

I bite off a finger...
Then one of his hands.
That's how I start eating
My gingerbread man.

I lick off the icing...
It's creamy and sweet,
And then I devour
His cute little feet!

Next are the buttons...
All shiny and red,
And last but not least—yum!
I BITE off his head!

Ode to A Fruitcake
An Original Poem

In the bleak midwinter
Sitting all alone,
In a breadbox on the shelf
Fruitcake hard as stone.
No one dares to taste it—
Or remove the bow
For we know that it was made
Oh so long ago.

First, they put in olives,
Kumquats by the pound.
Then they overbaked it
To a nice dirt brown.
Then into a plastic box
Impenetrable yet,
Gifted and re-gifted
For someone else to get.

Nancy bought it first of all
For my sister Kim.
Kim then gave it to our dad—
She'd nothing else for him.
Dad put it in the basement
For a year or two,
And now it's turned quite moldy
So I'm giving it to you!

Now in the bleak midwinter
Sitting all alone,
In a breadbox on the shelf
Fruitcake hard as stone.
No one dares to taste it
Or remove the bow
For we know that it was made
Oh so long ago.

THE TWELVE DAYS OF CHRISTMAS

Sung to: The Twelve Days of Christmas

On the first day of Christmas, I ate all I could see:
A cookie that's shaped like a tree.

On the second day of Christmas, I ate all I could see:
Two candy canes,
And a cookie that's shaped like a tree.

On the third day of Christmas, I ate all I could see:
Three lollipops,
Two candy canes,
And a cookie that's shaped like a tree.

On the fourth day of Christmas, I ate all I could see:
Four bags of chips,
Three lollipops,
Two candy canes,
And a cookie that's shaped like a tree.

On the fifth day of Christmas, I ate all I could see:
Five gummy worms!
Four bags of chips,
Three lollipops,
Two candy canes,
And a cookie that's shaped like a tree.

On the sixth day of Christmas, I ate all I could see:
Six frosted cupcakes,
Five gummy worms!
Four bags of chips,
Three lollipops,
Two candy canes,
And a cookie that's shaped like a tree.

On the seventh day of Christmas, I ate all I could see:

Seven popcorn garlands,

Six frosted cupcakes,

Five gummy worms!

Four bags of chips,

Three lollipops,

Two candy canes,

And a cookie that's shaped like a tree.

On the eighth day of Christmas, I ate all I could see:

Eight malted milk balls,

Seven popcorn garlands,

Six frosted cupcakes,

Five gummy worms!

Four bags of chips,

Three lollipops,

Two candy canes,

And a cookie that's shaped like a tree.

On the ninth day of Christmas, I ate all I could see:
Nine gooey clusters,
Eight malted milk balls,
Seven popcorn garlands,
Six frosted cupcakes,
Five gummy worms!
Four bags of chips,
Three lollipops,
Two candy canes,
And a cookie that's shaped like a tree.

On the tenth day of Christmas, I ate all I could see:
Ten chocolate Santas,
Nine gooey clusters,
Eight malted milk balls,
Seven popcorn garlands,
Six frosted cupcakes,
Five gummy worms!
Four bags of chips,
Three lollipops,
Two candy canes,
And a cookie that's shaped like a tree.

On the eleventh day of Christmas, I ate all I could see:
Eleven chewy caramels,
Ten chocolate Santas,
Nine gooey clusters,
Eight malted milk balls,
Seven popcorn garlands,
Six frosted cupcakes,
Five gummy worms!
Four bags of chips,
Three lollipops,
Two candy canes,
And a cookie that's shaped like a tree.

On the twelfth day of Christmas,
my mother gave to me:
A BIG Alka-Seltzer—for the:
Eleven chewy caramels,
Ten chocolate Santas,
Nine gooey clusters,
Eight malted milk balls,
Seven popcorn garlands,
Six frosted cupcakes,
Five gummy worms!
Four bags of chips,
Three lollipops,
Two candy canes,
And a cookie that's shaped like a tree!

POP
POP
FIZZ
FIZZ

CHOPSTICKS

Sung to: Chopsticks

*(To help you sing this song, we have capitalized the words
and syllables you should emphasize.)*

I wish we USED chopsticks FOR Christmas DIN-ner.
It'd BE much more FUN than a FORK and a KNIFE...Do we
HAVE to use NAP-kins and SAY "please" and "THANK you"?
No GRUNT-ing or BURP-ing, not FOR us to-NIGHT!

It's MUCH more FUN to USE our FIN-gers, and
BLOW some BUB-bles, and LICK the PLATE.
We HAVE to SIT up STRAIGHT and PRO-per—
No EL-bows LEAN-ing—these RULES I HATE!

I want to PLAY with the TOYS Sant-a BROUGHT me.
I WANT to get OUT of these PRI-ckly CLOTHES...but I'll
SIT like a PRIN-cess and SNEAK the dog GREEN beans.
It's MY lit-tle SE-cret that NO-bo-dy KNOWS!

CHRISTMAS CHARACTERS!

WHAT'S THAT SMELL?

Sung to: Jingle Bells

What's that awful smell?
It's been getting worse all day.
Just like sweaty shoes,
It just won't go away!

You need a shower now—
Maybe even two!
Rub-a-dub right in the tub
That smell right off of you!

Oh! Jingle bells—Rudolph smells!
Needs a bath today!
Oh, how stinky Blitzen is—
Please turn and go away—hey!

Jingle bells—Rudolph smells!
Reindeer are so ripe!
Better clean the herd right now
Before it's Christmas night!

SANTA'S PANTS ARE FALLING DOWN

Sung to: London Bridge Is Falling Down

Santa's pants are falling down,
Falling down,
Falling down.
Santa's pants are falling down,
'Cause he's thinner!

OOPS!

He worked out at Rudolph's gym,
Rudolph's gym,
Rudolph's gym.
Then he made some vegetables
For his dinner.

Santa's looking fit and trim,
Fit and trim,
Look at him!
He is healthy as can be!
He's a winner!

QUIET, PLEASE!!!

Sung to: It's Raining, It's Pouring

The story
Was boring.
Now Rudoph
Is snoring.
Mrs. Claus read
Him to bed
Now he's asleep till the morning.
The bed and
The room shake.
It sounds just like
An earthquake!
Tried counting sheep,
But still no sleep
With all the racket he makes!

Z-Z-Z-Z

"COOL" SANTA

Sung to: The Alphabet Song

Who's that coming—can it be?
Santa sure looks hip to me!
He just pierced his ear and nose.
Bought himself some cool new clothes.
But my guess is that he'll be
Grounded soon by Mrs. C!

LOST OUT WEST

Sung to: Home on the Range

Excuse me, old chap,

But do you have a map?

'Cause I'm lost and I can't find my way.

I've no time to spare.

Gotta get these gifts there.

'Cause tomorrow will be Christmas day.

I don't wanna whine,

And I'm hoping the children won't mind,

But come Christmas next,

I am calling FedEx!

To deliver to homes I can't find.

REINDEER DANCE

Sung to: Old MacDonald Had a Farm

REINDEER ONE:
Don't you dare step on my hooves
E-I—E-I—OUCH!
You're clumsy and can't dance at all!
You're making me a grouch!

REINDEER TWO:
With a two-step here

REINDEER ONE:
NO—a two-step THERE!!

REINDEER TWO:

Here a step . . .

REINDEER ONE:

THERE a step!

REINDEER TWO:

Don't you love to two-step?!

REINDEER ONE:

Don't you dare step on my hooves
E-I—E-I—OUCH!

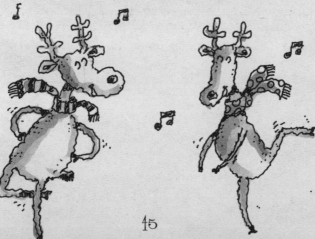

HOLIDAY
HEADACHES

DING-DONG

Sung to: Here We Come A-Caroling

Here we come a-caroling to spread some Christmas cheer!
Open up your doors! Come outside so you can hear!
'Cause we've practiced all day singing "Jingle all the way,"
And we think that we almost have the harmony just right.
This is not meant to be a silent night!

Here we come a-caroling around the neighborhood.
Though we love performing, our voices aren't so good.
But we sing cheerfully, though we mostly sing off-key,
And the neighbors all say our notes are painful to the ear,
"Go away, and don't come again next year!"

LETTER TO SANTA
An Original Poem

Santa, here's my Christmas list—
There's much I want to say.
I promise I've been good all year
In each and every way.

But, Santa, here's my problem—
For try hard as I might,
I cannot send this letter
'Cause I don't know how to write.

GET ME TO THE MALL IN TIME!

Sung to: *Take Me Out to the Ball Game*

Take me out to see Santa!
Take me out to the mall!
I've just completed my Christmas list.
Want to make sure that there's nothing I missed,
So let's rush, rush, rush to go see him.
Please, can I be first in line?
'Cause just 10—9—8 days remain
Till it's Christmastime!

THE DAY AFTER CHRISTMAS

Sung to: A Bicycle Built for Two

Santa, Santa, feelin' so sad and blue.
After Christmas, there isn't much to do.
My toys are already broken,
So here is what I'm hopin'
I'll start my list of things I missed
And next year want to get from you!

TIME FLIES

Sung to: Old King Wenceslas

Can't believe December's here.
Time is really flying
Mistletoe is hanging, and
Christmas gifts we're buying.

Seems we barely started school.
Halloween went so fast.
Dragged Thanksgiving turkeys out,
Leftovers are gone at last.

Christmas snuck up on us all.
There's so much to do now.
I could use an extra week—
Maybe even two now.

Can I have a bit more time?
I don't want to beg here,
But I still can't seem to find
One last Easter egg—oh, dear!

There's a Hole in My Stocking

Sung to: There's a Hole in My Bucket

There's a hole in my stocking, dear Santa, dear Santa.
There's a hole in my stocking, dear Santa, a hole.

Then fix it, dear Billy, dear Billy, dear Billy.
Then fix it, dear Billy, dear Billy, fix it!

With what should I fix it, dear Santa, dear Santa?
With what should I fix it, dear Santa, with what?

With bubble gum, dear Billy, dear Billy, dear Billy.
With bubble gum, dear Billy, just fix it with gum!

I just lost my front teeth, dear Santa, dear Santa,
So I cannot chew it, dear Santa, not me.

Use an air pump, dear Billy, dear Billy, dear Billy,
To blow up the bubble gum, dear Billy, a pump.

The pump's in the cellar, dear Santa, dear Santa.
The pump's in the cellar, the cellar downstairs.

       Then go to the cellar, dear Billy, dear Billy.
       Then go to the cellar—go downstairs right now!

But it's cold in the cellar, dear Santa, dear Santa.
It's cold in the cellar, dear Santa, so cold.

       Then put on some stockings, dear Billy, dear Billy.
       Then put on some stockings, some stockings, dear Bill.

But there's a hole in my stocking, dear Santa, dear Santa.
There's a hole in my stocking, dear Santa, a hole!!

Joy For a Day

Sung to: Joy to the World

Won't take a bath . . . or brush my hair,
I will . . . not make . . . my bed!
Don't feel like getting dressed today.
Don't care what anyone will say.
It's Christmas, for goodness sake . . .
So don't bug me, give me a break . . .
And for breakfast, for bre-eak-fast, I'd like some cake!

STRING OUT!

Sung to: Camptown Races

Christmas lights are all in knots
Uh-oh!
Uh-oh!
These are ones that Dad just bought
Oh, what will he say?

Supposed to put them up
On the Christmas tree
But now they're wrapped around my neck
Please get them off of me!!

ONSTAGE WITH A MANGER

Sung to: Away in a Manger

Onstage is a manger with shepherds around.
Some donkeys and sheep sit nearby on the ground.
I'd hoped to play Mary, the star of the play.
Instead, I'm the "Star" who has no lines to say.

My costume is itchy—the stage lights are hot.
I feel like a dork standing glued on this spot.
I wave at my parents. They both look so proud.
My brother is eating some lint off the ground.

The angels start singing. Their music's not sweet.
The organist's music fell under his seat.
But when the whole room begins singing this song,
I suddenly find myself joining along. . . .

"Away in a manger, no crib for a bed . . ."
The words that I'm singing swirl 'round in my head.
They make me feel lucky for all that I've got:
A home and a family that loves me a lot.

SHOW AND TELL

Sung to: The First Noel

The worst show-and-tell
That I ever did see
Was the one after Christmas
In Room 23.

All the kids brought to class
The worst gifts they'd received—
A collection of junk
That you would not believe.

Show-and-tell . . . show-and-tell
Where we all could dwell . . .
On gifts that none of us liked very well.

There were ugly purple socks
And some long underwear,
And pajamas with pictures
Of stupid ol' bears

And a book that told you how
You could clean up your room,
And it came in a set
With a dustpan and broom.

Show-and-tell…show-and-tell
Gifts that aren't so swell
Put them on ebay
And maybe they'll sell!

DAD'S CHRISTMAS PROJECT

Sung to: I've Been Working on the Railroad

Dad's been putting toys together
All through Christmas day.
"Some assembly required,"
That's what all the boxes say.
Tools are scattered all around him—
Plastic and metal lie about,
But which pieces fit together
He can't figure out!

First he was amazed.

Then he got confused.

Where is this part used and ho—o—ow?

He takes off his specs.

This is too complex.

He might need some Kleenex now.

Someone go and get him some pliers—

Someone grab a hammer now plea-ea-ea-ease!

Someone check the drawer 'cause the boxes

don't include bat-ter-ies.

Dad is fuming. . . .

Oh, my! What did he just say?

"TIME OUT" for talking that way—ay—ay—ay!

Mom's turn—watch her save the day.

All the toys are ready—hooray!!

Let's play!

O CHRISTMAS TREE

Sung to: O Christmas Tree

O Christmas tree
O Christmas tree
Your needles you are losing.

O Christmas tree
O Christmas tree
It's really not amusing.

Dad always picks the cheapest tree—
A sadder sight you'll never see.

Oh well, we love
You anyway—
Just wish we did the choosing.

LET'S GO HOME!

Sung to: Bill Bailey, Won't You Please Come Home

Can't we go home—you promised!
Can't we go home?
We've been here much too long
My toys are waiting for me
The TV's on
And staying here is wrong!

Remember how last evening
We made a pact?
We'd only stay till six.
And—holy cow!
It's seven now!
Come on—you promised—let's go home!

JUST PLAIN
SiLLy

CHRISTMAS "WRAP"

An Original Rap Song

YO YO YO YO—HO!
HO HO HO HO—YO!
CHRISTMAS IS HERE, YEAH!
BRING ON SOME CHEER, YEAH!

YO YO YO YO—HO!
LET'S HAVE SOME CO-COA!
FROM FAR AND NEAR, YEAH,
OUR FRIENDS ARE HERE, YEAH!

SANTA IS CO-MIN'
AND SONGS WE'RE HUM-MIN'
CHRISTMAS IS HERE, YEAH!
BEST TIME OF YEAR, YEAH!

O YARMULKE

Sung to: Come Light the Menorah

O yarmulke, o yarmulke, it fell on the floor–a.
The wind picked it up, and it blew out the door–a.
Mom will be so angry—hope she doesn't see!
If I cannot find it, NO gelt for me!!

HOLE-Y MOLE-Y CHRISTMAS CRAFTS

Sung to: Jolly Old St. Nicholas

Lost another tooth today—
This year, I've lost ten.
They could make a really cool
Christmas ornament . . .

Or I could just use them to
Make a brand-new wreath,
Or to change the mistle-toe
Into mistle-teeth!

NOT YET CHRISTMAS VACATION

Sung to: Row, Row, Row Your Boat

Child:
Snow, snow, snow all night!
Wouldn't that be cool?
Then tomorrow maybe they'd
Have to cancel school.

Mom:
No, no, not tonight.
There's too much to do.
Sending out our Christmas cards
And shopping just for you.

Child:
Oh, snow, go away!
I misunderstood . . . but
After Mom has bought my gifts,
Come back, if you could!

MERRY KISS–MUS

An Original Poem

Meet me under the Mouse-le-toe
We can hug like this!

I much prefer the Moose-le-toe . . .
And a great big Moose-le kiss!!
Giving a big kiss with great big moose lips!

WHAT'S THAT COMING DOWN THE SLOPES?

Sung to: Hark! The Herald Angels Sing

See the elephants on skis,

Trunks a-flapping in the breeze.

Shushing down the bunny trail,

Passing Peter Cottontail.

Oh, what style and oh, what gra-ace
And at such a rapid pa-ace!
Who'd have thought such gorgeous turns
Could have been made by pachyderms?
That's not all . . . now look and see . . .
Snowboarding hippos on a spree!

SNOW DAY!

Sung to: Yankee Doodle

Wake up, Mom, and look outside!
Last night we had a snowstorm.
Can I go and play outside
If I dress so I stay warm?

Mom, I put my snowsuit on,
Buttoned up my sweater,
Put some warm socks on my feet
And dressed up for the weather.

I'll collect a lot of snow
And make a great big snowman.
Maybe build a snow house, too,
Just like an Eskimo can!

Mom, I put my snow boots on,
Buttoned up my sweater.
Got my hat and mittens, too,
And dressed up for the weather.

Now I'm bundled head to toes
And dressed for late December,
But just as I step outside
There's one thing I remember...

Mom, I really need your help!
Please don't think I'm naughty.
Help me get these clothes off quick...
I have to use the potty!

CELEBRATE THE Season

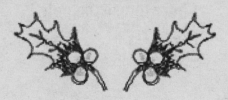

O BAGEL

Sung to: Dreidel Song

My mom gave me a bagel.
I left it out all night.
And when I woke this morning,
I could not take a bite.

O bagel, bagel, bagel—
I had to tell the truth
'Cause when I tried to eat it,
I almost broke my tooth.

O bagel, bagel, bagel—
At least as hard as clay.
Oh well, it's good for hockey—
Let's go outside and play!!

A SIMPLE CHRISTMAS WISH

Sung to: Twinkle, Twinkle Little Star

Twinkle, twinkle Christmas star
Shining brightly from afar.
You've led kings who lost their way
Toward their goal on Christmas day.
All I ask is with your light
Please lead Santa here tonight.

WARM THOUGHTS ABOUT KWANZAA

Sung to: Angels We Have Heard on High

Hanukkah has come and gone.
Yesterday was Christmas dawn.
But my heart's still filled with song,
So I'll sing out loud and strong. . .

Kwa-a-a-a-a-a-a-a-a-a-a-a-a-a-a-a-a-an-zaa
Everyone start humming. . .
Kwa-a-a-a-a-a-a-a-a-a-a-a-a-a-a-a-a-an-zaa
Keep those presents co-o-o-ming!

In Swahili, "Kwanzaa" means
Join our "first fruits" gathering.
But right now, no fruits will grow
'Cause outside it's ten below!
Kwa-a-a-a-a-a-a-a-a-a-a-a-a-a-a-a-a-an-zaa
In this snow, what harvest?
Kwa-a-a-a-a-a-a-a-a-a-a-a-a-a-a-a-a-an-zaa
Maybe snow peas wou-ould be best!

NEW YEAR'S RESOLUTIONS

Sung to: Auld Lang Syne

I'll make my bed, pick up my clothes,
And I'll brush my teeth each night.
I'll walk the dog and comb my hair,
And I promise not to fight.

Oh, can't I please stay up tonight
And raise a New Year's cup?
With apple juice we'll toast the year.
Can't you please, oh please, wake up?

THE DAY AFTER

Sung to: Silent Night

Ne-ew Year's day . . . what a slow day.
Stayed up late . . . now I'll pay.
Football's blaring upon the big screen.
Mom says that I'm too young for caffeine.
So, I turn and I cre-ep . . . back to my room . . .
for more sleep!